)6

1 1

Toasts and Short Speeches

Time-saving books that teach specific skills to busy people, focusing on what really matters; the things that make a difference – the *essentials*. Other books in the series include:

After Dinner Speaking

Making the Father of the Bride's Speech

Speaking in Public

Responding to Stress

Succeeding at Interviews

Moving House with Feng Shui

Making Your Money Grow

Making the Best Man's Speech

Making Great Presentations

Making the Most of Your Time

For full details please send for a free copy of the latest catalogue.
See back cover for address.

The things that really matter about

Toasts and Short Speeches

John Bowden

ESSENTIALS

Every effort has been made to identify and acknowledge the sources
of the material quoted throughout this book. The author and
publishers apologise for any errors or omissions, and would be
grateful to be notified of any corrections that should appear in any
reprint or new edition.

Published in 2000 by
How To Books Ltd, 3 Newtec Place,
Magdalen Road, Oxford OX4 1RE, United Kingdom
Tel: (01865) 793806   Fax: (01865) 248780
email: info@howtobooks.co.uk
www.howtobooks.co.uk

British Library Cataloguing in Publication Data.
A catalogue record for this book is available from
the British Library.

Edited by Alison Wilson
Cover design by Shireen Nathoo Designs
Cover copy by Sallyann Sheridan
Produced for How To Books by Deer Park Productions
Typeset by Anneset, Weston-super-Mare, Somerset
Printed and bound by Hillman Printers, Frome, Somerset

NOTE: The material contained in this book is set out in good faith for
general guidance and no liability can be accepted for loss or expense
incurred as a result of relying in particular circumstances on
statements made in the book. Laws and regulations are complex and
liable to change, and readers should check the current position with
the relevant authorities before making personal arrangements.

ESSENTIALS *is an imprint of*
How To Books

Contents

Preface

To most of us gatherings of family and friends are for special occasions: the 18th birthday celebrations, the silver wedding, the engagement party, Christmas festivities, and even great-grandma's 100th birthday – all to be remembered for years to come . . . and with a bit of luck, treasured.

Whatever the occasion, a toast or short speech makes it that extra bit special, if for no other reason than it provides you with an opportunity to say the things you would like to say at other times, but never do. You may find it too hard to say how much you appreciate your parents or your children, for example, and so you never say it. A family speech provides you with the golden chance to express your true feelings.

There are a number of old things which we are well rid of – London pea-soupers, the Berlin Wall, flared trousers and too many others to mention – but there are still other things that we would be foolish to let slip away. The tradition of making toasts and short speeches at social gatherings is one of them.

Anniversary dinners, reunions, retirement parties, all need something said well. Too often we think it's only when addressing outsiders that we need to be at our oratorical best. Not so! The first place is amongst family and friends.

John Bowden

1 Preparing and Delivering a Speech

At a family gathering, everyone is likely to be familiar with the background and character of the people involved. Use this information to make a warm, personalised speech.

things that really matter

1 **GETTING THE TONE RIGHT**

2 **CHOOSING YOUR MATERIAL**

3 **PUTTING IT ACROSS**

This first chapter will establish a set of ground rules that you should *always* apply when called upon to propose a toast or make a short family speech. The remainder of the book will supply you with a rich selection of ideas, one-liners and quotations which you can use or adapt for toasts and speeches at particular types of social gathering, be they formal or informal, joyous or sad.

Too many people, in my experience, strive to become over-eloquent when they address family and friends. Quoting long, flowery passages from famous speeches or poems, they try to emulate the oratorical excellence of Nelson Mandela, Martin Luther King or Winston Churchill and wind up sounding like pompous, stuffed shirts.

Effective speakers speak from the heart, use plenty of anecdotal material about the person or persons whom they are toasting, and include a few short memorable lines, jokes and quotes like those in this book.

① GETTING THE TONE RIGHT

Family speeches should be entertaining, inspiring and should include a tribute to one or more of your family or friends. The tone of your speech should be:

- **Optimistic:** This is not the time to share your personal woes, paint a gloomy picture of the present or offer dire predictions about the future. Leave your soap box at home.

Always look on the bright side of life!

- **Emotional:** You should feel free to display strong personal feelings. However, you *must* be genuine. False heartiness, cheap sincerity and – worst of all – crocodile tears will all be obvious to an audience.

Relate a couple of stories that illustrate your heartfelt feelings.

- **Enlivened with humour:** Inject some humour into your speech. The degree of levity depends very much upon the occasion and upon your personality. You do not need to be a stand-up comedian, indeed you should not be. But you must allow the humorous side of your personality to shine through.

Include some humour in every speech you make.

② CHOOSING YOUR MATERIAL

Don't expect to create a speech in ten minutes. Think about what you are going to say as early as possible, brood over it, sleep on it. Every pensive reflection will pay dividends when the time comes to speak your thoughts out loud to your audience.

Have a theme

In the case of an anniversary speech your theme could well be the couple's life together. A best man's theme is likely to be the recent marriage, while the theme of a speech at a reunion might be friendship. As you prepare your speech, have fun and by all means go off at occasional tangents, but make frequent trips back to your core theme in order to keep it all on track.

Tell them what they want to hear

The family speech is one occasion when you can really go to town – jokes, stories, quotes, anecdotes (especially treasured family memories) always go down well with loving parents and grandparents. Then simply add a few funny or serious lines, quotes and toasts from this book that you feel will be particularly appropriate to the occasion.

All your intimate confessions, witty observations, perceptive one-liners, amusing anecdotes and profound insights into the state of the world must be meaningful and relevant to your audience.

Much of the material that can be used at one kind of gathering can often be adapted to suit other situations. If you going to toast a relative's promotion at work, refer also to the section on graduations and examination success – because each of these occasions are celebrations of *achievement*. If you are going to speak at a retirement party – take a look at the chapter on birthdays as well. If you are searching for lines suitable for a wedding speech, don't ignore the section on anniversaries.

Foster group spirit

Your aim should be to create social cohesion and good

feelings. Make your audience feel proud to be members of this family. Remind them of the values and experiences they share ('Here's to our house and home; where there's a world of strife shut out, and a world of love shut in'). Talk about the kind of things they talk about. Concentrate on things that bind them together.

The vital thing with a tight-knit group of family and friends is to foster group spirit, to make a few references only they will understand, so that right from your first few sentences you reinforce the message that they are part of a special group.

Don't outstay your welcome

Don't suffer from the illusion that you can make your speech immortal by making it everlasting. Audiences today do not have the patience of inveterate watchers of county cricket. They have been programmed to expect and respond to soundbites, and they won't be afraid to chivvy you if you go on too long: 'Come on, son, the salad's getting cold!' 'Get on with it, dad, we're going on holiday in June!'

Get a good beginning and a good ending; and get them close together. Always stop before your audience wants you to. The point of satiation is reached very soon after the peak of popularity.

Prepare your script

The best talkers are those who are most natural. They are easy, fluent, friendly and amusing. No script for them. How could there be? They are talking only to us and basing what they say on our reactions as they go along. For most of us, however, that sort of performance is an aspiration rather than a description. Our tongues are not so honeyed and our words are less winged. We need a script.

But what sort of script? Cards? Notes? Speech written out in full? It's up to you. There is no *right way* of doing it. Here is a simple method favoured by many speakers:

- Write the speech out **in full**.

- **Memorise** the opening and closing lines and **familiarise** yourself with the remainder of the speech.

- **Summarise** the speech on one card or one sheet of paper using **key words** to remind you of your **sequence** of jokes, anecdotes, quotations, toasts and so on.

The main advantage of this method is that the speaker will not only be sure to cover everything he or she wants to, but also will come across as a natural and spontaneous speaker who is not merely reciting a prepared speech.

③ PUTTING IT ACROSS

It is exceedingly difficult to discuss style and technique in general terms, since the ability to be entertaining and 'hold an audience' is such a personal business. However, there are certain 'rules' and guidelines which appear to be universal. Here they are:

Make the speech 'yours'

Did Elvis, Sinatra and Johnny Rotten all sound the same singing *My Way*? Of course not. The artist makes the crucial difference. So, too, does the speaker.

What you say is so much more important than *how* you say it. A speaker without a powerful or melodious voice can register just as convincingly as a great orator as soon as the audience tunes into the fun and caring behind his or her words.

If you offer your homage, your humour and your heart to any audience, they cannot resist.

We all have *some* abilities and talents. Don't hide your light under a bushel. Have you any funny faces, impersonations or mannerisms of speech which infallibly convulse friends and relatives at parties? Whatever individual characteristics you have that are special to you should be nurtured and cultivated and worked on, for it is those personal and unique quirks of appearance, personality and expression that will mark you out as a speaker with something different to offer. And that is never a bad thing.

Be conversational

Sitting at leisure, with family and friends, your conversation will be naturally relaxed and chatty, because that is the language of easy communication. When you make a family speech to the same people your delivery should remain unaffectedly relaxed and chatty.

If you 'put on an act', you will be perceived as phoney, boring, or lacking in personality. As a result, you won't come over well. Certainly you may need to speak a little louder or make other concessions to accommodate the needs of your audience, but, in essence, nothing in your delivery style should change.

Casual conversation is not constructed in a literary way. You do not always finish your sentences. You repeat yourself. You use ungrammatical constructions – but you are obeying a different set of rules. You are obeying the rules of effective spoken communication which have been learnt, instinctively, down the ages. Don't abandon these rules when you make a speech or propose a toast.

The key then is to recognise what you are doing when you 'get it right' and achieve any successful communication, be it formal or informal, business or social, and then stay with it in any given situation, regardless of the stress level.

Be sincere

C.S. Forrester reminds us that 'Words spoken from the full heart carry more weight than all the artifices of rhetoric'.

You should feel free to display strong personal feelings when you speak.

Speaking from the head and the heart is sure to bring to the moment an appropriately sentimental touch. For instance, if you have just given your daughter away, ask yourself: Do I really want family and friends to know every last detail of her Saturday morning tap dancing lessons, or do I want to share something profoundly meaningful and joyous in our otherwise crazy world? Well, which would you prefer to hear?

Be friendly

All right, so you can't stand Uncle Andy and Auntie Flo. But this is not the time to air your grievances or cause family strife. Are there any subjects that must be avoided, such as your sister's iffy new boyfriend or big brother's recent brush with the law? Tread carefully and don't embarrass anyone.

Be enthusiastic

Remember that this is a live, one-shot deal. You have a great opportunity to tell friends and relatives – and to show them – how you really feel. Grasp it with both hands. Don't hold back. Give it plenty of wellie.

Try to involve *everyone* as you speak. The poor folks at the back will become more and more alienated if you appear to be having a private party with your mates at the front. Give everyone the benefit of your big blue eyes and flashing smile once in a while.

Be heard

Finally, even the most moving, inspirational or humorous speech in the world will count for naught if people can't hear you. You can make sure you are heard by everyone in the room, without shouting or straining, simply by:

● speaking a little louder than you usually do

● keeping your head up

● opening your mouth wider than during normal speech

● using clearer consonants

● slowing down.

You must be audible. If you are not, all else is lost.

2 Anniversaries

The best way to make sure you always remember your wedding anniversary is to forget it just once.

Not every anniversary is a milestone calling for a customised speech and toast, but every anniversary certainly deserves some type of mini-speech and toast. Here are some lines, quotes and toasts that can fit virtually any anniversary occasion. You can use these verses and thoughts as the foundation for your toast and, with a bit of adaptation and personalisation, you can come up with a perfect salute to any anniversary.

YOUR ANNIVERSARY

This speech is usually made by the husband.

General guidelines

- Be sober, sentimental and sincere.

- Don't be afraid to share your genuine emotions.

- Lighten your speech with occasional touches of gentle humour.

  'Here is to loving, to romance, to us.
  May we travel together through time.
  We alone count as none, but together we're one,
  For our partnership puts love to rhyme.'

  'My dear, we have been through much together, and although we are not as young as we once were, I recall the words of Ira Gershwin who wrote, "The memory of all that – No, no! They can't take that away from me".'

'I know of no better definition of love than the one given by Proust: "Love is space and time measured by the heart".' (Gian-Carlo Menotti)

'I'll love you, dear, I'll love you
Till China and Africa meet,
And the river jumps over the mountain
And the salmon sing in the street.' (W.H. Auden)

'All to myself I think of you,
Think of things we used to do,
Think of the things we used to say,
Think of each happy bygone day,
Sometimes I sigh and sometimes I smile,
But I keep each olden, golden while
All to myself.' (Wilber D. Nesbit)

'Happy marriages begin when we marry the one we love, and they blossom when we love the one we married.'

'I have more happy memories than if I were a thousand years old.'

'God gave us memory so that we may have roses in December.' (J.M. Barrie)

'May the warmth of our affections survive the frosts of time.'

'Here's a health to the future;
A sigh for the past;
We can love and remember,
And hope to the last,
And for all the base lies

That the almanacs hold
While there's love in the heart,
We can never grow old.'

THEIR ANNIVERSARY

This speech is usually made by the oldest friend of the married couple.

General guidelines

- Mention the anniversary and what else you may be doing or plan to do to commemorate the occasion.

- Include a few amusing anecdotes involving the couple.

- Express your confidence/hope that there will be many more anniversaries to celebrate.

  'A dance never seems too long when you have the right partner.'

  'Do not resist growing old – many are denied the privilege.'

  'Love is not a matter of counting the years . . .
  it's making the years count.'

  'Here's to you both –
  a beautiful pair,
  on the birthday of your love affair.'

  'To the happy couple.
  Anniversaries will come and anniversaries will go,
  but may your happiness continue forever.'

'To your coming anniversaries –
may they be outnumbered only by your coming
pleasures.'

'Here's to the husband,
And here's to the wife;
May they remain lovers for life.'

'You will never be old
With a twinkle in your eye,
With the Springtime in your heart
As you watch the Winter fly.
You will never be old
While you have a smile to share,
While you wonder at mankind
And you find the time to care.
While there's magic in your world
And a special dream to hold,
While you can laugh at life,
You never will be old.' (Iris Hellelden)

However, some anniversaries are that extra bit special. So here is some additional material that could be pressed into service when celebrating the really biggies. The verses suggested for Silver, and Ruby Anniversaries can easily be adapted for other anniversaries too.

Twenty-fifth anniversary

'It's your Silver Anniversary and we just want you to know
That you were in the perfect place when Cupid shot his bow.
For all these years you've been in love and that sure says a lot.

'Cause 25 years ago today, you were considered a very long shot!'

Fortieth anniversary

'Your friends and relatives are gathered here to celebrate your Ruby Anniversary.
You must have gotten married when the bride was only three.
'Cause you don't look your ages . . . you look very youthful
And I mean it when I say that . . . I am absolutely truthful.'

Fiftieth anniversary

'With 50 years between you
And your well-kept wedding vow.
The Golden Age, old friends of mine,
Is not a fable now.'

And, finally, here's a humorous one that can be adapted for any old-timers:

'(X) score and (Y) years ago
You both said "I do".
How anyone could last that long.
I haven't got a clue!'

3 Birthdays

Birthdays are a time to celebrate – the memories of days gone by, the joys of the moment, and the dreams of tomorrow.

Birthday speeches are chiefly for the middle aged and elderly. Young people generally don't want to hear speeches and toasts. But 18th and 21st birthday parties are exceptions. At these celebrations it is customary for a parent or guardian to say a few words.

The character of a birthday speech will naturally depend greatly on the character and age of the person whose birthday is being celebrated – often mickey-taking for the 40-year old; respectful for the 80-year-old. Concentrate on the birthday boy's or birthday girl's good qualities, but avoid lavish praise or you may cause embarrassment and appear insincere.

General guidelines

- Express your affection and good wishes for the individual.
- Include a couple of humorous anecdotes.
- Focus on the other person rather than yourself.

GENERAL

'Here's to you. No matter how old you are, you don't look it.'

'May you live to be 100 years old, with one extra year to repent.'

'To wish you joy on your birthday

And all the whole year through,
For all the best that life can hold
Is none too good for you.'

'Many happy returns of the day of your birth;
Many blessings to brighten your pathway on earth
Many friendships to cheer and provoke you to mirth;
Many feastings and frolics to add to your girth.'

'To your birthday, glass held high,
Glad it's you that's older – not I.'

COMING OF AGE

'Key to the door: 18, 21, or five, if both parents are
working.' (Mike Barfield)

'One good thing about being 18 is that you are not
experienced enough to know that you can't possibly
do the thing you are doing.'

'When I was one and twenty
I heard a wise man say,
"Give crowns and pounds and guineas
But not your heart away;
Give pearls away and rubies,
But keep your fancy free."
But I was one and twenty
No use to talk to me.' (A.E. Housman)

'Towering in the confidence of twenty-one.' (Dr Samuel
Johnson)

'Remember that as a teenager you are in the last stage of your life when you will be happy to hear that the phone is for you.' (Fran Lebowitz)

'If youth be a defect, it is one that we outgrow only too soon.' (James Russell Lowell)

'Keep true the dreams of thy youth.' (Friedrich von Schiller)

MIDDLE AGED

'Middle age is when:

- you begin to exchange your emotions for symptoms (Bob Monkhouse)

- you can't work out how to set the timer on the video (Victoria Wood)

- whenever you go on holiday, you pack a sweater' (Denis Norden).

'So now you're really over the hill
Like a barrel falling over Niagara.
Hey, don't you despair,
You've still got some hair
And for the rest there's a pill called Viagra.'

'He doesn't look like he's 40 . . . but he used to.'

'When you've reached a certain age and think that a face-lift or a trendy way of dressing will make you feel ten years younger, remember – nothing can fool a flight of stairs.' (Denis Norden)

'The trouble with being middle aged is that what should stay down comes up . . . and what should stay up goes down.'

'Another candle on your cake?
Well, that's no cause to pout,
Be glad that you have strength enough
To blow the damn thing out.'

ELDERLY

'You know you're getting old when:

- your idea of hot, flaming desire is a barbecued steak (Victoria Fabiano)

- the candles cost more than the cake (Bob Hope)

- you can make the wrinkles that you see in the mirror disappear just by taking off your glasses' (George Burns).

'Another year older?
Think of it this way;
Just one day older
Than yesterday.'

'Age does not depend upon years, but upon temperament and health. Some people are born old, and some never grow old.' (Tyron Edwards)

'The gardener's rule applies to youth and age:
When young "grow wild oats", but when old, grow sage.'
(H.J. Byron)

'The man never grows old who keeps a child in his heart.'

'While we've youth in our hearts, we can never grow old.' (Oliver Wendell Holmes)

'When your friends begin to flatter you on how young you look, it's a sure sign you're getting old.'

'You've heard of the three ages of man – youth, age, and "you're looking wonderful".'

'About the only way to stay young is to live honestly, eat sensibly, sleep well, work hard, worship regularly, and lie about your age.' (E.C. McKenzie)

'Age is really a question of mind over matter. If you don't mind, it doesn't matter.'

'To be 70 years *young* is far more cheerful and hopeful than to be 40 years *old*.'

'I'm as old as my tongue and a little older than my teeth.' (Jonathan Swift)

'Every morning I read the obituaries in *The Times*. If I'm not in it, I know I'm still alive.'

'To me, old age is always five years older than I am.'

4 Christenings and Confirmations

A christening should be a solemn yet happy occasion.

CHRISTENINGS

In the Christian religion, the baptism of a new-born represents the soul of the child being committed to the Lord. Etiquette states that the first speech should be made by the baby's godfather or a family friend. This is followed by a few words from the parents. Finally, if the grandparents aren't also the godparents, one or both of them may also want to make a contribution.

General guidelines

- Speeches should be light-hearted and cheerful in character.
- The godfather should include a compliment or two to the mother and father.
- If the godfather is a grandfather, he could recall an amusing incident about his son or daughter when *THEY* were babies.
- The reply to the Toast to the Baby, made by the baby's father, should include a positive reference to the godparents, if there are any.

GODFATHER OR FAMILY FRIEND

'May s/he enjoy a long life, wealth and happiness.'

'I love to gaze upon a child;
A young bud bursting into blossom.' (Charles S. Calverley)

'The youth of a nation are the trustees of posterity.'
(Benjamin Disraeli)

'A thing of beauty is a joy forever:
Its loveliness increases'. (John Keats)

'The smallest children are nearest to God, as the smallest
planets are nearest the sun.' (Jean Paul Richter)

'A child is not a vase to be filled, but a fire to be lit.'
(Francois Rabelais)

'A baby will make love stronger, days shorter, nights
longer, money tighter, home happier, clothes shabbier,
the past forgotten, and the future worth living for.'

'Babies are bits of stardust blown from the hand of God.
Lucky the woman who knows the pangs of birth for she
has held a star.' (Larry Barretto)

'People who say they sleep like a baby usually don't have
one.'

'You can learn many things from children. How much
patience you have, for instance.'

'A new life has begun,
Like father, like son.'

'Like one, like the other,
Like daughter, like mother.'

'Here's to the baby – woman to be,
May she be as sweet as thee.'

'May this be the last bath at which your baby cries.'

'A mother's pride, a father's joy!' (Sir Walter Scott)

'A toast: To quiet nights and dry nappies!'

FATHER

'Ladies and gentlemen, I must apologise on behalf of my son, who regrets he is unable to reply to your kind words himself.'

'Father of fathers, make me one,
A fit example for a son.' (Douglas Malloch)

'Two's company. Three's the result!'

'Nappy birthday!'

'Congratulations, love, we all knew you had it in you.'

GRANDPARENTS

'Grandchildren are gifts of God.
It is God's way . . .
Of compensating us for growing old.'

'Small traveller from an unseen shore,
By mortal eye ne'er seen before,
To you, good-morrow.' (Cosmo Monkhouse)

'A baby is something a woman carries inside her for nine

months, in her arms for three years and in her heart till the day she dies.'

'We have become a grandmother.' (Lady Thatcher)

CONFIRMATIONS

Confirmation is another rite of passage followed by the Christian religion, representing the acceptance of young people as members of the church body. Speeches should be more serious, but fairly general in nature, wishing the individual a long life, happiness, and many blessings. Here are a few other appropriate lines that would help set the right tone:

'The truth shall make you free.' (John 8:32)

'No longer a child
You're a soldier of God
So pray right now
That He finds you a job.'

'Through biblical passages that they have learned,
It is time to celebrate (name) getting confirmed.
Praise God they now have faith in the Lord;
We can now celebrate as one in accord!' (Maggie Ness)

'As this child enters the membership of the church, let us remember Paul's words to the Galatians, "As we have therefore opportunity, let us do good unto all men."' (Galatians 6:10)

5 Christmas and New Year

Special holidays call for special toasts,
and December is the home of the year's
most special holidays.

Many families have their own holiday toasts that have been passed down from generation to generation. If your family doesn't currently have a heart-warming toast to fall back on, I'm sure you can find one from the following selections. Tradition has to start somewhere!

CHRISTMAS

Unless you happen to be the Queen (thanks for buying the book, Ma'am), *your* Christmas message should be short, simple, jovial, convivial, and totally in keeping with a time of festivities.

General guidelines

- Express warm wishes for the season.

- The degree of religious content of your speech (if any) should depend on the nature of your family's religious beliefs (if any).

- Keep it light. As poet W.H. Davies put it: 'Christmas has come, let's eat and drink – This is no time to sit and think'.

'At Christmas play and make good cheer
For Christmas comes but once a year.'

'Here's to the holly with its bright berry.
Here's to Christmas, let's make merry.'

'Drink a brandy, stir the toddy,
Merry Christmas everybody.'

'Here's to the day of good will, cold weather, and warm
hearts!'

'I know I've wished you this before
But every year I wish it more.
A Merry Christmas!'

'Here's wishing you more happiness
Than all my words can tell,
Not just alone for Christmas
But for all the year as well.'

'Christians awake! Salute the happy morn,
Whereon the Saviours of the world was born!'

'I heard the bells of Christmas day
Their old, familiar carols play.
And wild and sweet
The words repeat
Of peace on earth, goodwill to men.'
(Henry Wadsworth Longfellow)

'The best Christmas gift of all is the presence of a happy
family all wrapped up with one another.'
(E.C. McKenzie)

'Heap on more wood! The wind is chill
But let it whistle as it will.
We'll keep our Christmas merry still.'
(Sir Walter Scott)

'Joy to the world – and especially to you.'

'The past is past, but I hope the present is what you wanted.'

'May you live as long as you Wish, and have all you Wish as long as you live. This is my Christmas Wish for you.'

'Happy Christmas!'

NEW YEAR

New Year is a time of celebration, of the renewal and beginning of a brand new year. Like Janus, the Roman god of doors after whom the month of January is named, your speech should both look backward and forward. The passing of the old year and the coming of the new should be celebrated with a toast preceded by a brief speech of proposal.

General guidelines

- Remember that this is a time of hope, humour, optimism and rededication.

- Emphasise success, health and happiness to everyone present.

- Toast absent friends, wish a speedy recovery to anyone ill, and say a few positive words about anyone close who passed away during the previous twelve months.

    'Here's to the bright New Year
    And a fond farewell to the old:
    Here's to the things that are yet to come
    And to the memories that we hold.'

'In the year ahead,
May we treat our friends with kindness
and our enemies with generosity.'

'May all your troubles during the coming year last as
long as your New Year's resolutions.'

'Whatever you resolve to do,
On any New Year's day.
Resolve to yourself to be true
And live – the same old way.'

'Absent friends – though out of sight, we recognise them
on this New Year's Eve with our glasses.'

'One swallow doesn't make a summer . . . but it breaks a
New Year's resolution.'

'I resolve this year to shed some pounds,
I'm going to lose some weight,
But the dinner sure looks good today,
I guess the weight can wait.'

'Another year is dawning! Let it be
For better or for worse, another year with thee.'

'Year's end is neither an end nor a beginning but a going
on, with all the wisdom that experience can instil in us.'
(Hal Borland)

'If you resolve to give up smoking, drinking and loving,
you don't actually live longer; it just seems longer.'
(Sir Clement Freud)

'New Year's Day is every man's birthday.'
(Charles Lamb)

'Ring out the old, ring in the new,
Ring, happy bells, across the snow:
The year is going, let him go;
Ring out the false, ring in the true.'
(Alfred, Lord Tennyson)

'The Old Man's dead. He was okay, maybe,
But here's a health to the brand new baby.
I give you the year 200X!'

'Should auld acquaintance be forgot,
And never brought to min?
Should auld acquaintance be forgot
And days of auld lang syne.
For auld lang syne, my dear,
For auld lang syne,
We'll tak'a cup o'kindness yet,
For auld lang syne.' (Robbie Burns)

'Happy New Year!'

6 Engagements and Weddings

The most conspicuous of all family toasting occasions are engagements and weddings.

Getting engaged should be wildly romantic and the engagement party should be a joyous indulgence. All the speeches and toasts should reflect a happy, carefree, upbeat mood. Speeches at the ensuing wedding reception should be a little more considered. While every wedding speech should include a few sincere, optimistic and entertaining words, there are some subtle differences in the messages expected from the main speakers.

That's why this chapter concentrates on wedding speeches. However, any of the lines, quotes and toasts that follow would work equally well at an engagement party as well as at a wedding reception (but don't use the same ones at both!).

WEDDINGS

The main purpose of every wedding speech is to propose a toast or to respond to one, or to do both. This is the traditional three-step programme:

1. **The bride's father (or mother, close family friend, other relative or godfather):** proposes to the bride and groom.

2. **The bridegroom (possibly with the bride):** responds to the toast and then proposes a second toast.

3. **The best man (or best girl):** responds to the second toast on behalf of the bridesmaids (and any other attendants).

However, things have changed a great deal both socially and culturally over the last few years, and now it is perfectly acceptable for other people to speak instead of or as well as these. It all depends on the personal attitudes, circumstances and backgrounds of the newlyweds.

FATHER OF THE BRIDE

This speech should contain some positive thoughts about the couple and about love and marriage in general. Your aim should be to strike a nice balance of humour, emotion and seriousness.

General guidelines

- The father of the bride is expected to say a few reasonably sober, sensitive yet witty words.

- Thank everyone for coming to celebrate your daughter's big day.

- Say a few affectionate words about the bride and groom.

- Stress the joy you and your wife have had in bringing up your daughter.

- Relate one or two amusing or serious incidents from her childhood.

- Talk of the pleasure you have found in getting to know your new son-in-law and his parent(s).

- Offer some (possibly amusing) thoughts about love and what makes a happy marriage.

- Declare your confidence that the bride and groom will make all the effort needed and will not be found wanting.

- Propose a toast to the bride and groom.

  'To the bride and groom:
  There are only two lasting bequests we can hope to give
  our children. One of these is roots, the other is wings.'

  'It is written:
  "When children find true love,
  parents find true joy."
  Here's to your joy and ours,
  from this day forward.'

  'Here's to the bride and groom!
  May you have a happy honeymoon,
  May you lead a happy life,
  May you have a pile of money soon,
  And live without all strife.'

  'Here's to the husband and here's to the wife,
  May they be lovers for the rest of their life.'

  'Let us toast the health of the bride;
  Let us toast the health of the groom,
  Let us toast the person that tied the knot,
  Let us toast every guest in the room.'

  'The love you give away is the only love you keep.'

  'I toast you on behalf of myself.
  And I toast you on behalf of my spouse.
  We're glad you married our daughter.
  And got her out of the house.'

'Much happiness to the newlyweds from the oldlyweds.'

BRIDEGROOM

The bridegroom responds to the toast to the bride and groom making it clear he is also speaking on behalf of both of them (unless his bride is going to say a few words as well). He must convey that he is conscious of the meaning of the occasion and its importance to him. Times and manners change, but human nature and the human condition do not. It is not demeaning, and certainly not shaming, to be emotionally honest and patently sincere.

General guidelines

- The bridegroom's speech is expected to be middle of the road.

- Thank the previous speaker for his or her kind remarks and good wishes, and, if applicable, for laying on this reception.

- Thank your parent(s) for the help and support provided over the years.

- Tell everyone that you are the luckiest man in the world.

- Thank everyone for attending – and their generous gifts.

- Say a few complimentary words about the bridesmaids before proposing a toast to them.

  'How do I love you? Let me count the ways,
  I love you to the depth and breadth and height
  My soul can reach.'
  (Elizabeth Barrett Browning)

'You know, my love, you are a thief . . . because you have stolen my heart.'

'Because I love you truly,
Because you love me, too,
My very greatest happiness
Is sharing life with you.'

'Here's to my mother-in-law's daughter,
Here's to her father-in-law's son;
And here's to the vows we've just taken,
And the life we've just begun.'

'Do you love me
Or do you not?
You told me once
But I forgot.'

'Today I have married my best friend.'

BRIDE

Today, quite rightly, more women than ever literally want to speak for themselves. The bride's speech, once a rarity, is undoubtedly here to stay.

General guidelines

Follow the general advice proffered to the bridegroom. You may wish to emphasise that your marriage will be a wonderful partnership of equals.

'I know I cannot change you,
And you know you won't change me.
Together let's go hand in hand,
Towards the best that life can be.'

'You are my husband now,
And I am your wife.
I plan to be with you,
For the rest of my life.'

'Being loved by you makes me feel protected but not smothered,
Challenged but not threatened,
Directed but not controlled,
Wanted but not possessed.
You are the one with whom I am not afraid to become "we".'

'People destined to meet will do so, apparently by chance, at precisely the right moment. We were destined to meet and destined to spend the rest of our lives together.'

'It has been said that true love is like a ghost. Everyone talks about it but few have seen it. Here's a toast to my husband, we are among the happy few.'

BEST MAN

Rather oddly, it is traditional for the best man to respond to the toast to the bridesmaids. All that is required is acknowledgement of the toast, a few light-hearted words about the bridegroom – with a couple of compliments and congratulatory remarks woven in.

General guidelines

- Respond to the toast to the bridesmaids.

- Remember that tact is essential.

- Never embarrass the bride or knock the institution of marriage.

- Alternate little digs at the bridegroom with genuine compliments to the bride and groom.

  'May the love you share forever remain as beautiful as the bride looks today.'

  'May all your hopes and dreams come true, and may the memory of this day become more dear with each passing year.'

  'May your joy be as bright as the morning, and your sorrows but shadows that fade in the sunlight of love.'

  'Here's to one marriage . . . and to many anniversaries.'

  'May your love be as endless as your wedding rings.'

  'Here's to the bride and here's to the groom,
  And here's to the bride's father who paid for this room.'

  'May all your tomorrows be promises come true.'

  'Here's to true love, may it always be spoken.
  Here's to true friendship, may it never be broken.'

  'Down the hatch to a wonderful match.'

7 Funeral Orations and Eulogies

Funerals are a time of grieving, sadness and personal reflection. They are also a time to celebrate the life of the departed.

While a funeral is a solemn occasion, it is also a time to look back to happier days, to share memories with those who knew, liked or loved the deceased. Rarely has this been done more effectively and movingly than during the eulogy scene featured in the film *Four Weddings and a Funeral*.

General guidelines

As this occasion is different in nature from any other family gathering, the following advice is quite detailed and comprehensive:

- Funeral speeches, even in church, don't *have* to be religious. It is not necessary to rattle off a dozen scriptures and some 'woes' and 'yeas' and 'nays'.

- Polish and formality are not nearly as necessary at a funeral as sincerity and and genuine concern.

- Arrive early at the service, so that most of the people will arrive after you. This will give you a feeling of familiarity and control.

- Immediately express your grief over the loss – recognise how the family feel and let them know you feel the same. Express your gratitude for being there to your friends and family.

- Avoid going into specific details of the tragedy or illness.

- Show your respect and affection in a straightforward natural manner.

- Summarise your special association with the deceased. Share some close personal stories that present the deceased in a good or appealing light. Express some of the deceased's most intimate wishes and joys, as you knew them. Point out that of all things we all expect in life, the deceased got a fair share or more.

- Conclude on an inspiring note with gratitude for the deceased's contributions in life.

  'We are gathered here not to mourn the death of (deceased); we are gathered here to celebrate his life.'

  'We are gathered here today in the presence of (deceased's) family and his friends and his God to say that here was a life that demands notice . . . a life that exemplified kindness . . . a life that inspired emulation . . . a life that burned so that others' paths were lighted. He was the living proof of how fine a person can be.'

  'To be born a gentleman is an accident –
  To die one is an accomplishment.'

  'Too soon (deceased) has left us. Our lives will be empty in places that his energy once filled.'

  'I can do no better than repeat the words of Samuel Johnson who said: "It matters not how a man dies, but how he lives". Here's to our dear departed relative – to our dear departed friend – who lived life to its fullest.'

'(Deceased) gave us encouragement, time, laughter. Only the time is gone. The encouragement and the laughter will remain.'

'You can't control the length of your life, but you can control its breadth, depth and height.'

'In the words of composer Irving Berlin, "The song is ended; but the melody lingers on."'

'Memories, images, and precious thoughts
That shall not die, and cannot be destroyed.' (William Wordsworth)

'When one man dies, one chapter is not torn out of the book, but translated into a better language.' (John Donne)

'God is closest to those with broken hearts.' (Jewish saying)

'Those we love remain with us, for love itself lives on.
And cherished memories never fade because a loved one is gone.
Those we love can never be more than a thought apart
For as long as there is memory they'll live on in the heart.' (Anon)

'It is not the years in a life that counts; it's the life in the years. (Deceased) lived. We will miss him.'

'Death beckoned him with outstretched hand and whispered softly of an unknown land.

He took death's hand without fear. For God, who brought him safely here, had promised He would lead the way into Eternity's bright day.

For none of us need go alone, into the valley that's unknown. But guided by our Father's hand we journey to the Promised Land.

And as his loving, faithful wife, who shared his home and heart and life,

You will find comfort for your grief, in knowing death brought sweet relief.

For now he is free from all suffering and pain, and your great loss became his gain.

You know his love is with you still, for he loved you in life and always will.

For love like yours can never end, because it is the perfect blend

Of joys and sorrows, smiles and tears, that just grow stronger through the years.

So think of your loved one living above, no further away than your undying love.

And now he is happy and free once more and he waits for you at Eternity's Door.' (Anon)

'Do not stand at my grave and weep;
I am not there, I do not sleep.
I am a thousand winds that blow.
I am the diamond that glints on snow.
I am the sunlight on ripened grain.
I am the gentle autumn's rain.
When you awaken in the morning's hush.

I am the swift uplifting rush.
Of quiet birds in circling flight.
I am the soft stars that shine at night.
Do not stand at my grave and cry.
I am not there, I did not die.' (Anon)

8 Graduations and Examination Success

Graduations and other exam successes are big events in life. Celebrate them with a degree of fun in a first class speech.

In his later years, Winston Churchill was asked to address a group of graduates at Oxford University. Following his introduction, he rose, went to the rostrum, and said, 'Never, never, give up!' Then he took his seat. Like the great man, your aim is to craft a speech that is concise and memorable.

GRADUATIONS

General guidelines

- Congratulate the graduate on their academic achievements.

- Outline some obstacles and challenges they may face in the future.

- Aim for a fresh approach, avoiding clichés such as 'This is the first day of the rest of your life'.

  'A toast to the graduate – in a class by him/herself.'

  'Try to know everything of something, and something of everything.'

  'Congratulations on your achievement. Over the last three years you have spent 1,250 hours partying; 1,750 hours in the pub; 2,600 hours in the student union doing nothing; and almost 4.5 hours actually studying. We don't know how you did it but we're glad you did.'

'Today is the biggest day of your life;
It's yours and yours alone.
Now go out and tackle the world, my friend,
And pay back your student loan.'

'As Benjamin Disraeli once said, "A university should be a place of light, of liberty, and of learning". Today we toast your enlightenment, your liberation and your knowledge.'

'Shoot for the moon . . . even if you miss, you'll still be among the stars.'

OTHER EXAMINATION SUCCESS

General guidelines

- Offer your sincere congratulations.

- Lead the audience in an appreciation of the achievement of the individual.

- Mention the effort, time or expertise this distinction required.

- Express pride in the individual.

  'The foundation of every state is the education of its youth.' (Diogenes)

  'What we want to see is the child in pursuit of knowledge, not knowledge in pursuit of the child.' (George Bernard Shaw)

'Examinations are formidable even to the best prepared, for the greatest fool may ask more than the wisest man can answer.' (Charles Calab Colton)

'I've always treated the Ten Commandments as I would exam questions. You know, you must attempt no more than four of them.'

'The significance of a man is not in what he attains, but rather what he longs to attain.' (Kahlil Gibran)

'There is a great deal of difference between the eager man who wants to read a book, and the tired man who wants a book to read.' (G.K. Chesterton)

'Do not on any account attempt to write on both sides of the paper at once.' (W.C. Sellar and R.J. Yeatman)

'If genius is one per cent inspiration and ninety-nine per cent perspiration, you must stink!'

THE RESPONSE

It is not unusual for the graduate or exam-passer to say a few words to all the family and friends that have joined together to help him or her celebrate.

General guidelines

- Mention why your achievement was important to you, if appropriate.

- What is your driving force, your goal?

- Share the credit with any others who have contributed to your achievement, perhaps financially or through other support. However, don't make it sound like an Oscar-winning acceptance speech!

- Be modest; don't boast of all your efforts and accomplishments on the road to success.

- Display emotion appropriate to the occasion but avoid overexuberance.

- Thank your friends and relatives for caring enough about you and your success to attend.

  'To my parents. Thank you for your support, your help, and your money. I fully intend to pay back the support and help.'

  'A toast to my family and friends who join me in celebrating today. The more schooling that I receive and the more knowledge I attain only reinforce what I have known all along ., . . that you are the greatest gifts with which I have been blessed.'

  'It's hard to believe that three years ago I couldn't even spell education, and now I done got myself one.'

9 Mother's Day and Father's Day

'God could not be everywhere, so he made parents.' (Hebrew proverb)

Very often we tend to neglect the people closest to us because we just take for granted the fact that they will always be there. As we all know, a time will come when our loved ones will be in a place very far from us. For me it was Strangeways, but that is a story for another time. The lines in this chapter are ideal for Mother's Day and Father's Day, but they can be used to toast our dear parents in any place and at any time.

General guidelines
Or rather guideline, and it's this:

* Keep it very simple and one hundred per cent sincere.

MOTHER'S DAY

'Having a child makes you a mother, but loving and caring makes you a mum. Here's to you, Mum!'

'To Mother – may she live long enough to forget what little devils we used to be.'

'There is in all this cold and hollow world no fount of deep, strong, deathless love, save that within a mother's heart.' (Felicia D. Hemans)

'In the heavens above
The angels, whispering to one another,
Can find, amid their burning terms of love,
None so devotional as that of "mother".' (Edgar Allan Poe)

'To mum, who was like a comfortable quilt,
She kept us kids warm but never smothered us.'

'All that I am, or hope to be, I owe to my angel mother.'
(Abraham Lincoln)

'You may have a friend,
You may have a lover,
But don't forget,
Your best friend is your mother.'

'The mother's heart is the child's schoolroom.' (H.W.
Beecher)

'To the mother who bore me,
There's no one more bold,
She's dearer by far
Than all the earth's gold.'

'We have toasted our futures,
Our friends and our wives,
We have toasted each other
Wishing all happy lives:
But I tell you my friends,
This toast beats all others,
So raise your glasses once more
In a toast to – our mothers.'

FATHER'S DAY

'A father is someone you look up to no matter how tall
you grow.'

'Anyone can be a father, but it takes someone special to be a dad.'

'You're a kind of father figure to me, Dad.'

'In the words of Cole Porter, "My heart belongs to Daddy".'

'Father. May the love and respect we express toward him make up, at least in part, for the worry and trouble we caused him.'

'What a father says to his children is not heard by the world, but it is heard by posterity.'

'When I was a boy of fourteen, my father was so ignorant I could hardly stand to have the old man around. But when I got to twenty-one, I was astonished at how much he had learned in seven years.' (Mark Twain)

'Dad, you paid for my schooling,
And bought me my first car,
Now I'm going to France,
So I say "Au revoir!" '

'Let's raise a glass to the man who raised us.'

'Here's to my father. If I can become but half the man he is, I will have achieved greatness.'

10 New Jobs and Promotions

The only place you will find sucess before sweat, toil and tears is in a dictionary.

Getting a new job or being promoted are among the most important personal achievements in our life. And, as such, they deserve to be recognised by family and friends. The best personal achievement speeches, of course, are customised just for the recipient. Start with a general toast or a celebrity quote and build to a personalised toast to highlight the recipient's achievements.

General guidelines

- Lead the audience to appreciate the achievement of the individual.

- Mention the effort, time or expertise this new job or promotion required.

- Express pride in the individual.

NEW JOBS

'They say that success is getting what you want, and that happiness is wanting what you get . . . You've already made it to my definition of success. Our wish is that you'll have all the happiness you expect and deserve in your new job.'

'All work and no play makes Jack a dull boy,
And all play and no work makes Jack a mere toy.' (Maria Edgeworth)

'When you attend an interview arrive nice and clean, be friendly but not too familiar, speak clearly (and in the right language). Be decisive, answer clearly and concisely, if you don't know . . . say so. Try to enjoy yourself and leave the interviewer with a good impression. Most importantly, don't forget to ask: 'Whom do I make the cheque out to?' (Simon Bond)

'The closest to perfection a person ever comes is when he fills out a job application form.'

'When (name) was interviewed for his job, his supervisor asked him if he could make tea. (Name) said, "Yes"." And can you drive a fork lift truck?" his boss continued. "Why?" asked (name), "How big is the teapot?" '

'(Name's) boss says he's a miracle worker. It's a miracle if he works.'

'(Name) asked me to give his application form a quick once over before he sent it off. It was a good thing he did. Where he was asked, "Length of residence at present address", he had replied, "About 20 metres – not counting the garage." '

PROMOTIONS

'See the conquering hero comes!
Sound the trumpets, beat the drums!' (Dr Thomas Morell)

'The world has a habit of making room for a man who knows where he's going. You've got the talent and determination to get anywhere you want to go. We're just glad (company) made room for you there.

Congratulations on your promotion.'

'The best careers advice is "Find out what you like doing best and get someone to pay you while you're doing it." (Katharine Whitehorn)

'The will to win is not nearly as important as the will to prepare to win.'

'Success is a journey, not a destination.' (Ben Sweetland)

'Plough deep while sluggards sleep.' (Benjamin Franklin)

'After a concert, a fan rushed up to famed violinist Fritz Kreisler and gushed: "I'd give my whole life to play as beautifully as you do". Kreisler replied, "I did".'

'For every criticism you make of someone's job performance, make sure you give the person four compliments.'

'Be nice to people on your way up because you'll meet them again on your way down.'

'Never turn down a job because you think it's too small, you don't know where it can lead.' (Julia Morgan)

'Here's to becoming the top banana without losing touch with the bunch.'

THE RESPONSE

The achiever is then expected to say a few words to their family and friends who have come to help them celebrate their good news.

General guidelines

● Follow the same advice proffered to new graduates and other exam-passers on page 49.

'The toughest thing about success is that you've got to keep on being a success.' (Irving Berlin)

'It took me 20 years to become an overnight success.'

'It's a sobering thought . . . that when Mozart was my age he had been dead for two years.' (Tom Lehrer)

When I left (previous employer), they gave me this reference: "Any employer who gets Mr (name) to work for him will be very lucky".

'The reward of a thing well done is to have done it.' (Ralph Waldo Emerson)

● 'Whatever women do they must do twice as well as men to be thought half as good. Luckily, this is not difficult.' (Charlotte Whitton)

11 Retirements

Retirement is a wonderful time; nothing to do all day and if you leave it half done it doesn't matter.

At no time are people more economical with the truth than *before* an election, *during* a war and *after* a fishing trip. But speakers come pretty close at retirement parties! Therefore, be particularly careful as there is only a very thin line between genuine warmth of expression and embarrassing sycophancy.

Find out one or two interesting or amusing incidents from the working life of the retiree to give your speech real content. Who better to ask than their long-standing colleagues and friends? But don't simply chronicle their career path. The participants want to celebrate, not listen to a CV. If you don't know already, try to find out something about their leisure activities and hobbies, too. Finally, why not talk to the retiree beforehand to find out what *they* want to hear?

THEIR RETIREMENT

General guidelines

- Use generosity generously. Express your admiration and appreciation for the retiree's hard work and dedication over the years.

- Expand on pleasant personality traits and any notable job successes.

- Use anecdotes from the person's work life to make it unique and personal.

- Comment positively on future plans.

- Wish the person well.

- Be sincere, uplifting and inspirational, but avoid flowery, overblown sentiment.

- Avoid negative remarks about age, health or future finances.

If you sense that the guest of honour is delighted to be spending more time with the family, and you *know* he or she is a good sport, sections of your speech can be quite abrasive:

'Retirement does not mean that the employee is no longer wanted or needed by the company. In this case though, it happens to be true.'

'There's two things (name) loved about this job . . . Saturdays and Sundays.'

'Retirement can be a happy time, a pleasant time, a joyous time, unless you are married to (name).'

'I can see you patterning your retirement after the words of Grouch Marx, who said: "I'm an ordinary sort of fellow: 42 around the chest, 42 around the waist, 96 around the golf course, and a nuisance around the house".'

On the other hand, if you sense it's really a case of redundancy dressed up as early retirement, or if you think the retiree is dreading leaving work, the occasion will need to be handled with far more tact and sensitivity. The tenor of your speech should be:

'To your retirement: A well deserved reward for a job well done.'

'To a man who now has the freedom to do all the things he spent the last 35 years dreaming of doing.'

'The next time we sit in yet another traffic jam on our way to work, you'll be sitting at home, enjoying a leisurely breakfast.'

'While one finds company in himself and his pursuits, he cannot feel old, no matter what years he may be.' (Amos Bronson Alcott)

'In proposing this toast to (name), I am reminded of the words of Bob Monkhouse who said: "I went to the doctor last week. He told me to take a hot bath before retiring. "That's ridiculous." said Bob, "it'll be years before I retire!" Well, (name), it's bath time.'

'You can rise when you want,
Do as you please,
Work in the garden,
Or just sit at ease.
Your options are many,
Everyday will inspire,
For a new life begins
On the day you retire.' (Phyllis Ellison)

YOUR RETIREMENT

General guidelines

- Thank your immediate family for their support, particularly during any difficult times.

- Don't dwell on any negative aspects of your job(s).

- Comment on future plans in a positive, upbeat manner.

Only you know what you *really* think about being put out to grass. But however you feel, try not to come over as twisted and bitter (it's not your family's fault!).

'I am interested in leisure the way a poor man is interested in money. I can't get enough of it.' (Prince Philip)

'Retirement is the time of life when you can stop lying about your age and start lying about the house.'

'When a man retires and time is no longer a matter of urgent importance, why do his colleagues generally present him with a watch?' (R.C. Sherriff)

'I'm planning out my retirement just like I planned out each working day. Show up. Have a cup of tea. Read the paper. See what happens next.'

'In the words of historian Arnold Toynbee, "To be able to fill leisure intelligently is the last product of civilisation". I'm looking forward to a very civilised retirement.'

If you are the retiree, paint a bright picture of your future – whatever you really may think about it!

12 Reunions and Surprise Parties

*The nuclear family has experienced fallout,
making the demand for family reunions and
surprise parties greater than ever.*

The traditional average family of mum, dad and two or three children no longer exists, if it ever did. Today, families often come with a mum, dad, step-mum, step-dad, siblings, step-siblings, and even step-step siblings. And at the same time an ever increasing number of these families are scattering themselves all over the country – and often all over the world.

Given these sociological and demographic trends it is hardly surprising that family reunions and surprise parties are becoming more and more popular and poignant occasions.

General guidelines

- Make the audience feel proud to be members of this special family.

- Talk about significant family events (hatches, matches and despatches) that have occurred since you all got together last.

- Be inclusive but give a special mention to anyone who has made a particular effort to attend.

Let's face it, most surprise parties aren't. So if you are headed for a gathering of the clans, planning a reunion, or expecting to be the 'victim' of a 'surprise' party, you may wish to arm yourself with one or two of the following lines.

THE FAMILY

'To my family: those who know me best and, for some reason, still love me.'

'May we be loved by those we love.'

'Here's to family, the people who treat us the best and the ones we grumble at the most.'

FRIENDS

'Here's to Eternity – may we spend it in as good company as this night finds us.'

'May the friends of our youth be the companions of our old age.'

'Old friends are scarce,
New friends are few;
Here's hoping I've found
One in each of you.'

'Here's to all of us!
For there's so much good in the worst of us
And so much bad in the best of us,
That it hardly behoves any of us,
To talk about the rest of us.'

'Friendship: May differences of opinion cement it.'

ABSENT FRIENDS

'Some of our family and friends live a long way away and coundn't make it here tonight. (Name them.) Their presence would have added to our enjoyment of the festivities. But I am sure that they would want us to enjoy

ourselves just as much in their absence, and would ask
no more than that we make a brief pause to think quietly
of them for a few moments, and to drink in silence to –
Absent Friends.'

MOTHERS AND FATHERS

You'll find plenty of lines, quotes and toasts suitable for
mums and dads in Chapter 9. Here are some others that
would do nicely when talking about or to other esteemed
members of your illustrious tribe.

SONS

'To our son:
We gave you life,
We gave you clothes,
We gave you milk and honey.
Now you're on your own
We can't give you any more
'Cause mum and I spent all the money.

DAUGHTERS

'To our daughter:
We've watched you grow from a little girl,
To a beautiful woman of style.
We'd tell you this more often if
You came home once in awhile.'

BROTHERS

'When God created brothers
He made them thoughtful and kind.
When God created brothers,
He must have had you in mind.'

SISTERS

'For there is no friend like a sister

In calm or stormy weather;

To cheer one on the tedious way,

To fetch one if one goes astray.

To lift one if one totters down,

To strengthen whilst one stands.' (Christina Rossetti)

AUNTS AND UNCLES

'Here's health to you

And wealth to you

And the best life can give to you

And Life be long and good to you

Is the toast of your nieces and nephews to you.'

GRANDPARENTS

And how better to round off a little book on toasts and speeches than with a few choice words addressed to the elders of your clan? This delightful all-purpose toast is certain to make them smile.

'Let us raise our glasses

And then imbibe

To the wonderful couple

Who started this tribe.'

I'll leave you with this final thought: Keep all your family toasts and speeches short and simple. Stand up to be seen, speak up to be heard and shut up to be appreciated. Cheers!